Another

Cup

of

Devotion

by

Dee Parramore

To my husband
&
my sons,

You are
my
everything

Thank you! Thank you! Thank you!

When "**From Coffee Bean to Mustard Seed**" was published, I had no idea the reception it would receive. Little did I know that there would be requests for another book! I honestly thought it was a one-time blessing.

I was amazed at the number of copies ordered and that it was read in other countries, too! But, it was your wonderful comments of both the book as a whole and about particular devotions that you related to that was the most humbling of all.

I had prayed that the book would be an opportunity to share lessons that I learned during my personal study time. I now pray thanking God for allowing me that blessing (Philippians 1:3-4).

Now, here we are with "**Another Cup of Devotion**". The devotions in this book were written and texted after "**From Coffee Bean to Mustard Seed**" was published. They are in the same simplistic format, made to be quick and easy reads, but designed to direct you to the Bible for a more extensive study.

These devotions are simple lessons I learned and wisdom I gleaned while drinking my coffee in the mornings and studying my Bible. These are my personal Bible notes, but the *perfect* lessons and wisdom come directly from God Himself. Therefore, I urge you to read the verses in each devotion in its context. I used both ESV and NKJV.

Included in this book are challenges after each devotion. It may be a question or a short-term goal, but something that we can use in our growth as a Christian. After all, that is what is expected of us (2 Peter 3:18).

Go grab your Bible and another cup of coffee. Let's indulge in Another Cup of Devotion.

DEVOTIONS

T h i n g s   t o   R e m e m b e r

Of the utmost, love. I want to be loving. Whether I get it in return or not, love! Not just the "easy" love my family, love my neighbor kind of love. I really want to love the annoyed clerk that threw all my groceries into my basket like they were on fire. Love!

If I am full of love, I just might share some joy! Being around a happy person usually lightens up my day, if even for a little while. It can be contagious. Like cooling an angry clerk by wishing her a better rest of her day. It's a peace from remembering to love.
Love, joy and peace!

I'll have to practice though. A lot! I'll have to be patient, suffering long and working hard at it. But it'll be worth it! I'll start with being kind and good to everyone. Yes, even to that clerk!

My faithful endurance in being kind and good needs to include myself, as well. If I practice self-control, I'll be more gentle, therefore, better at being good and kind. This can be done! It must be done. By this they will know I am a disciple of Christ (John 13:35).

And it all starts with love!

*****

"But the fruit of the Spirit is love, joy, peace, patience, kindness, goodness, faithfulness, gentleness, self-control; against such things there is no law."
Galatians 5:22-23

Challenge: With love, intentionally bear fruit of the Spirit toward someone or in a situation. Write down your result:

_____

_____

In Control

It's easier to...

Submit (James 4:7-8; John 5:26-29)

Encourage (Philippians 2:1-5; 1 Thessalonians 5:11)

Learn (Matthew 11:28-30; 1 John 5:1-3; Psalm 119:7)

Be courageous (Psalm 31:24; Ephesians 6:10)

Be bold (Proverbs 28:1; Ephesians 3:11-12; Hebrews 13:6)

Sacrifice (Romans 12:1-2; 1 Peter 2:19-21)

Love (John 15:12; 1 John 4:10-11)

...when you know Who's in control.

*****

"Turn to me and be saved, all the ends of the earth! For I am God, and there is no other. By myself I have sworn; from my mouth has gone out in righteousness a word that shall not return: 'To me every knee shall bow, every tongue shall swear allegiance.'"
Isaiah 45:22-23

Challenge: Choose one (or more) from the list above and allow the Lord to be in control. Write down your choice and how He was in control.

_____

_____

_____

_____

I n f l u e n c e

Early 2019, Drew Brees issued a statement expressing the same sentiment and frustration as the New Orleans Saints fans after a bad officiating call during a football game. Rather than staying angry, he suggested they pour their passions and emotions into their families and communities instead, inspiring a positive outlook. Being the city's hero, reactions were immediately positive and uplifting, vowing to follow through.

That was the influence of one person!
One's influence can make or break another.
One's actions can destroy another's hope. Or it can pick another up from despair.
One's words can tear down another's esteem. Or it can strengthen another's confidence.
One's influence can stall or motivate, enrage or encourage, shatter or repair, confuse or redirect focus. Think about it.

My influence is in direct relation to whom I'm dependent upon:
"he [the devil] was a murderer from the beginning, and does not stand in the truth, because there is no truth in him. When he lies, he speaks out of his own character, for he is a liar and the father of lies." John 8:44.

OR

"Finally, all of you, have unity of mind, sympathy, brotherly love, a tender heart, and a humble mind. Do not repay evil for evil or reviling for reviling, but on the contrary, bless, for to this you were called, that you may obtain a blessing." 1Peter 3:8-9.

The perfection of One has destroyed the evil of another for all eternity. But until the Perfect One returns, the evil one will still try to bring me down as many times as I allow him to. I must solely depend on the Perfect One to influence those around me.

*****

"And the Lord's servant must not be quarrelsome but kind to everyone, able to teach, patiently enduring evil, correcting his opponents with gentleness. God may perhaps grant them repentance leading to a knowledge of the truth, and they may come to their senses and escape from the snare of the devil, after being captured by him to do his will."
2 Timothy 2:24-26

Challenge: Write out a plan to use your Christian influence, whether in word or deed, to influence someone toward Christ and His saving gospel (Colossians 3:17).

_____

_____

_____

_____

_____

_____

_____

_____

Jonah

After spending three probably really disgusting, dark, tortuous days in the depths of a great fish praying, Jonah obeyed God's command. And Nineveh repented and was spared God's wrath. Jonah 3:10 could've been the "they lived happily ever after" ending to the book. But, instead, the Holy Spirit continued on with Jonah.

After Nineveh's repentance, Jonah was angry...again! This time at God's justice! Through a short-lived plant, God shared a small bit of His grace and mercy with Jonah. Then, the book ends with a question from God. That's it! No answer to the question. No explanation. No finality. Just a question.

I've read Jonah more than once. But this time, rather than wondering what happened to Jonah, I asked some poignant questions.
- Am I angry at sin or the sinner (Jude 21-23)?
- Do I want God to punish the wicked because I think they deserve it (Romans 12:19)?
- Will I run away from the Lord's command or go teach repentance? (Matthew 28:19-20)?
- Can my short-lived life testify of God's grace and mercy (Romans 5:15; Romans 6:23)?

Questions that only I can answer! The answers only I can explain.

*****

"The men of Nineveh will rise up at the judgment with this generation and condemn it, for they repented at the preaching of Jonah, and behold, something greater than Jonah is here."
Matthew 12:41

Challenge: Honestly answer the questions. Only you can.

I Will Weep

There's no wonder why Jeremiah is called the weeping prophet. His book is terribly heartbreaking and frustrating. I was reading it in the morning, but it would put me in such an awful mood. So I thought I'd read it in the evening, but that just depressed me. I considered not finishing the book, but I knew that wouldn't be fruitful or wise either.

Why is it so hard to get through this book? Then it hit me. Because I am in that book! I see *me* when I read it. Well, that hurts!

I have been Jeremiah, pleading with my wayward spiritual family to repent, but they refuse to submit (5:3). I have shared the Lord's love with others, but their hearts were too hard (9:24). I have prayed for open minds to listen to the saving gospel, but only heard their reply, "'Peace, peace', when there is no peace" (8:11). I weep with Jeremiah.

But, I have also been one of the stubborn people of God. I, too, have knowingly refused to attend worship because I was tired from the weekend (18:12). I, too, have let my personal time with the Lord take a backseat to my busy schedule (13:10). I, too, put the Lord aside believing all is fine and dandy (23:16-17). Again, I weep with Jeremiah.

The Lord kept His word with Jeremiah and with His lost people. He will keep His word with me, too. Will I weep with the lost (Luke 13:28)? Or will I joyfully weep when I hear, "Blessed are the dead who die in the Lord from now on. 'Yes', says the Spirit, 'that they receive rest from their labors, and their works follow them.'" Revelation 14:13

Challenge: Read the book of Jeremiah.

Orphans & Widows

The Holy Spirit through James said "Religion that is pure and undefiled before God the Father is this: to visit orphans (fatherless - KJV) and widows in their affliction, and to keep oneself unstained from the world." (1:27)

I found it interesting that He especially chose orphans and widows. Not the deaf and blind, or even the sick and hungry.

Ephesians 1:5 says that when I obeyed the gospel, I was adopted. Who else can be adopted? Orphans, the fatherless. So, before my spiritual adoption through the gospel, I was without the Father. Fatherless. An orphan.

Widows are ones whose spouses have died. Christ is the Bridegroom, His church is His bride (Rev. 21: 9, 27). He died for His bride, leaving her a widow.

But He specifically said *widows in their affliction*. Affliction is defined as distress or grief. The church is afflicted through persecution this side of eternity. Only the hope of being reunited with her Bridegroom for all eternity, where death shall part them no more, is comforting and brings her hope.

Jesus miraculously healed the blind, deaf, sick and hungry. There is no record of His interaction with orphans & widows. He left that work for me!

Visiting orphans is also teaching the gospel (Mark 16:15-16).
Visiting *widows in their affliction* is also encouraging my church family (1 Thessalonians 5:11-14).
Doing such is obeying His will, keeping myself *"unstained from the world"*.

*****

"If anyone loves me, he will keep my word, and my Father will love him, and we will come to him and make our home with him."
John 14:23

Challenge: Aim to accomplish each of these -

_____ visit a widow

_____ arrange a visit to a local orphanage, maybe with another member or with the youth group

_____ choose a member of your congregation and encourage him/her for a week or a month

_____ choose a neighbor, friend, co-worker and try to get a Bible study

Priestly Details

I'll admit that reading all the details of every single thing the Lord commanded Moses for His people to do and obey is a bit taxing. When I want to skip over it, I shamefully remind myself that He is patiently teaching me something (2 Timothy 3:16-17). With that in mind, I studied Exodus 29 this morning.

The Lord commanded Moses to consecrate Aaron and his sons for priesthood. Moses was given very specific and detailed instructions, down to the exact place where the consecration was to occur (29:4).

Since Christians are "a royal priesthood" (1Peter 2:9), there is relevance in this. Moses washed them with water then dressed them in the beautiful priests' clothing. After the Lord washed me in baptism, He then put on my beautiful priest clothing, Christ (Galatians 3:27).

Moses had to offer a bull as sin sacrifice for 7 days, but also 2 lambs had to be sacrificed, one in morning then one at twilight (vs. 35-41). Surely that *very* bloody process would have been remembered longer than morning till twilight. While the bull represented sin, the little lambs were just another bloody sacrifice (Hebrews 10:4). Only God's Lamb with **HIS** bloody sacrifice could take away my sins. Therefore, it is His Lamb's sacrifice that I must remember longer than morning till twilight.

In Genesis 22:13, the Lord provided a ram for Abraham as a sacrifice in place of his son, Isaac. Interesting that the blood of a ram was to be put on the right ear, right thumb, and right great toe of Aaron and his sons (vs. 20). Because of His providence (ram), I can listen (ear) to Him (Mark 9:7); grab hold (thumb) of my hope of Heaven (Hebrews 10:23); and stand firm (great toe) in His word (Gal. 5:1). All of which I could not do without those important parts.

This whole consecration had to be obeyed perfectly and completely for seven days (vs. 35-37) which is the same number that is representative of completeness and perfection throughout the Bible.

How wise is the awesome God of heaven! Perfect and Holy!

*****

"For by a single offering he has perfected for all time those who are being sanctified."
Hebrews 10: 4

Challenge: Read Hebrews 10:1-23

For He Was Afraid

"So he said to Jether his firstborn, 'Rise and kill them!' But the young man did not draw his sword, for he was afraid, because he was still a young man." Judges 8:20

The Lord told Gideon that He would give the Midianites into his hands. So he pursued and captured the two kings of Midian: Zebah and Zalmunna.

The Holy Spirit said that Jether was a young man. I can only imagine his internal conflict. He knew that his father was commanded by God to be the strong warrior to help Israel, but to actually use his own sword to kill the enemy?? I don't know how young Jether was at this point, but Gideon knew Jether was old enough to do it. The struggle was that he was not experienced enough to carry out that command. He needed help!

Not only was Gideon Jether's father by blood, but he was also his father in faith. They both were warriors for God. Jether, the young warrior, needed guidance, encouragement, faith, and leadership. Did Gideon provide that for young Jether? The Midianite kings were quick to pounce on the opportunity to mock Jether, "...for as the man is so is his strength" (vs. 21).

When I am a Gideon, I pray I am able to strengthen the young Jethers around me. When I am in a new situation to fulfill the Lord's command like Jether, I pray that my internal conflict fades and am strengthened to use my sword against the Lord's enemy. And I pray I NEVER pounce on the opportunity to mock the young Christians around me!

*****

"Now, we exhort you, brethren, warn those who are unruly, comfort the fainthearted, uphold the weak, be patient with all. See that no one renders evil for evil to anyone, but always pursue what is good both for yourselves and for all."
1 Thessalonians 5:14-15

Challenge: Choose a specific time frame and be someone's Jether. Write down your results.

_____

_____

_____

_____

_____

_____

_____

_____

_____

_____

_____

What's on my Table?

Generations after the building of the tabernacle, Solomon built a temple, a very magnificent, extremely beautiful, and grand temple. The place where the Lord's people went to worship Him, pray to Him, and be in awe of Him. The place where His people would commune with Him (1 Kings 6).

One of those times was the Passover. God's people would journey to Jerusalem to remember how He saved them from death. It was a yearly trek that covered many miles for some. Jesus and His family observed the Passover annually (Luke 2:41).

Now imagine the Savior from death and eternal punishment seeing and hearing the noises of a marketplace in His temple, year after year. Seeing the lack of respect, awe, and love of The Father. Hearing the clinking of their money, the bellowing of their oxen, and the bleating of their sheep.

To see these people, whom He so desperately wanted to have love Him (Luke 13:34), belittle and degrade His Father, and think only of selfish gain must have welled up a number of emotions through the years. He must've gone through hurt, insult, shame, embarrassment, then finally anger.

Overturning of the tables in His anger (John 2:13-16) couldn't have been a spur of the moment incident. After all, He overturned tables a second time before His death three years later for the same reason (Matthew 21:12). Year after year after year of seeing His people desecrating the command to worship.

This makes me reflect on my worship.

- Do I make melody in my heart or is it the bleating of disrespect?
- Is my breaking of bread taken in solemn gratitude or is it the bellowing sound of daydreaming?
- Is my cheerful giving as I purposed in my heart or the begrudged clinking of change?

*****

"But the hour is coming, and now is, when the true worshipers will worship the Father in spirit and truth; for the Father is seeking such to worship Him."
John 4:23

Challenge: With John 4:24 in mind, answer the questions.

My Hibiscus

I love everything about gardening. I love getting my hands in the dirt, watering and pruning the plants, then reaping the reward whether it's enjoying the flower blooms or eating the veggies. What I don't like about it are the bugs! Not all bugs are bad. Some are pollinators like bees. Some are beneficial little warriors like the ladybug that eat the bad bugs. But it's these pests that make gardening a real pain!

Pests come in from nowhere and can eat up tomato plants overnight, stealthily suck the life giving sap over time, or are simply the egg carriers of these pests. It's an ongoing battle that sometimes makes me want to dig it all up and burn it.

A few weeks ago, I had huge, vibrant flowers that were the size of my hands on my hibiscus tree. The next day I found aphids. How?! The tree lives in the lanai. I pruned the branch that was infected. That encouraged new growth. More blooms - yay! Well this morning, it was covered in aphids! I was so mad!! How dare those gross bugs make my tree look ugly! Branch by branch I cut, leaving just the main trunk and a few well established healthy branches.

As I angrily cut and tossed those branches into my water bucket of destruction, uttering curses to those wretched little aphids, I caught a faint glimpse of The Lord's wrath. At that moment, I thought about John 15. How many times has The Lord seen branches of His beautiful perfect Vine become infected by the "bad bugs"? These bugs, either sneaking in and destroying it overnight or maybe sucking the life giving gospel over time (Jude 1), has to get Him mad. How dare those gross bugs make His beautiful Vine look ugly!

Now, I have a very bare hibiscus tree with its few healthy branches patiently waiting for the new blooms. And I think about the final time the Lord will prune (2 Thessalonians 1). It motivates me to want to be well established in His Vine, patiently waiting for the beautiful promise of Heaven.

*****

"I am the true vine, and my Father is the vinedresser. Already you are clean because of the word that I have spoken to you."
John 15: 1, 3 ESV

Challenge: Read John 15 and Jude

The Buttress

This word would've sent my two boys into fits of giggles when they were little. Actually, it probably still could today. But its definition is different than their reason for laughing.

A buttress is a projecting support of stone or brick built against a wall; a source of defense or support. They are usually seen in old structures like castles, cathedrals, etc.

When Peter confessed Christ as the Son of God, the foundation of the church was firmly laid (Matthew 16:13-19). Jesus is the cornerstone upon which the rest is built (Ephesians 2:20). Without Christ, without the most important "brick", there is no church. With the same confession from others through the centuries, He is adding more "bricks" to His temple (Acts 2:47). This temple, His church, is His dwelling place on Earth (2 Corinthians 6:16).

So what does this have to do with the giggle-word? The buttresses of the Lord's temple (the church) is the projecting support of the structure, our projection of the church. In other words, our behavior (1 Timothy 3:15 ESV). If a buttress is unappealing, it can cause damage to the portion of its wall. We can change the beautiful curbside appeal of the church into a dump.

On the other hand, the buttresses could project to those looking on as a source of defense (2 Timothy 3:11), a place of strength (2Timothy 3:12-14). A place where the One True Living God lives with His people, a place that cannot be destroyed no matter how many attacks it endures (2Timothy 1:8-9,13-14).

How do I project His Kingdom? Do I stand for the truth (John 17:17)? Do I seek refuge in the Lord, my safe haven (Psalm 16:1)? Does my strength come from His power (Psalm 18:1-2; Romans 1:16)? It better!!

Challenge: How will you project the Lord's kingdom?

Onesiphorus

Peter, James, John (the beloved apostle), Paul, Stephen, Priscilla and Aquila. These are who are usually named when asked who is thought to be some of the greats in the New Testament.

I wouldn't hesitate to name them either. But while reading 2 Timothy recently, I now hope to be remembered as Onesiphorus was remembered by Paul. He had to have been *so* encouraging that the Lord saw fit for him to be named in the holy scriptures.

"May the Lord grant mercy to the household of Onesiphorus, for he often refreshed me and was not ashamed of my chains, but when he arrived in Rome he searched for me earnestly and found me— may the Lord grant him to find mercy from the Lord on that day!—and you well know all the service he rendered at Ephesus."
2 Timothy 1:16-18 ESV

He refreshed Paul, was not ashamed of his chains, searched earnestly and found him. And he served Paul.

*****

And I saw the dead, great and small, standing before the throne, and books were opened. Then another book was opened, which is the book of life. And the dead were judged by what was written in the books, according to what they had done.
Revelation 20:12 ESV

Challenge: Be Onesiphorus. Earnestly search for a "Paul" in chains and serve. Write your result.

_____

_____

_____

David and the Obstacles

The young shepherd, David, was appalled when Goliath defied God (1 Samuel 17:10,26). And he made sure Goliath understood his sin (vs. 45)!

I always wondered why the Lord made mention of the five smooth stones. Why specify "smooth"? Maybe because after that stone sunk into Goliath's forehead, no one could say it was because of the jagged edges cutting thru the skin. A smooth stone wouldn't be able to do that like a natural rough-cut rock could.

But I also wondered why David chose 5 stones. Did he think he'd miss his target on the first shot? Did he think one stone wasn't enough to kill him? Was he thinking that the stones would maim Goliath, then he'd go in to kill the Philistine? Whatever the reason, he knew that he would fight for the Lord, and the Lord would defeat the evil giant.

But in the process, David had a few challenges:
- his older brother basically told him to hush up and go home
- trying to convince the other soldiers to fight and then hearing their rejection
- trying to convince King Saul that the Lord will win
- not having armor that fit just right

There is nothing new under the sun (Ecclesiastes 1:9-10). I find myself appalled at the defiance of the worldly people I encounter and also face similar challenges:
- older/spiritually matured brother's discouragement at my request to fight for the Lord
- trying to encourage other soldiers of Christ to fight and then hearing their rejection
- convincing others that the Lord will win
- not having my entire armor of God fitting just right.

What did the man after God's own heart do?
- He threw off the armor that didn't fit.
       I, too, must throw off the armor of doubt and fear
       (Ephesians 2:10).
- David grabbed 5 smooth stones as a weapon.
       I must remember that I already have the Chief Cornerstone
       not some rough-cut rock (1Peter 2:7).
- David went out to fight absolutely convinced the Lord would win
the battle.
       If I'm going to sing this song, I'd better believe it:
       "The battle belongs to the Lord" (1Corinthians 15:57).

*****

"Who is this King of glory? The Lord, strong and mighty, the Lord, mighty in battle!"
Psalm 24:8

Challenge: Read 1 Samuel 17

In the Body

The divinity of Jesus was a fact I accepted because, well, that's what I've always heard. But reading Hebrews and thinking about mankind's relationship with God, I was able to really grasp it rather than simply hold it in my back pocket.

If sin separates man from God (Isaiah 59:2), then the face to face relationship between God and man ended after Adam sinned (Genesis 3:8-19). Man needed to get right with God. But how? Man cannot see God's face and live (Exodus 33:20).

God's glory is so magnificent, so brilliant, so awesome, thats it's too much for man to bear. When Moses spent time talking with the Lord, He had to cover his shining face in order to speak to the Israelites again (Exodus 34:29-35). How was man ever going to be in that face to face relationship again? Thankfully, the Omniscient had a plan (Ephesians 1:3-6).

God had to be covered in order to speak to us again (Hebrews 2:9,14,17). He covered His shining glory in the likeness of a man, Jesus, so that we can see Him (John 14:9-11) and actually live (John 3:13-17).

God Himself came to earth to teach us, as Jesus Christ (Matthew 1:23; 2 Corinthians 5:18-19), everything we need to know (2Peter 1:3), why we should love Him (1 John 4:19), and how to obey Him (Romans 6:1-4). He offered us an opportunity to accept His plea to live with Him (1Timothy 2:3-6).

When we obey Him, we put on Christ in baptism (Galatians 3:27). God can then see us in the body of Christ (Colossians 1:18, 24) just as we can see God in the body through Christ. Jesus is that door (John 10:2, 7, 9) that directly connects us to heaven. It is only through this entryway (John 14:6) that we are made right with Him (John 17:23) and enter into an eternal relationship with Him face to face.

*****

"Father, the hour has come; glorify your Son that the Son may glorify you, since you have given him authority over all flesh, to give eternal life to all whom you have given him. And this is eternal life, that they know you, the only true God, and Jesus Christ whom you have sent. I glorified you on earth, having accomplished the work that you gave me to do."
John 17:1-4 ESV

Challenge: Write down several of the ways Jesus glorified His Father. Choose one of those ways to glorify the Father this week.

One Language

On a recent mission trip, I was reminded of so many things. But one that stood out to me was the multiple languages. There were many dialects of this nation's language that even within this country, the natives sometimes couldn't understand each other.

I had a translator to help me and to guide me, whether in personal Bible studies or in my everyday activities. I was dependent on my translator, my helper. She knew the three languages necessary to help me talk to people and to tell me what they were saying. She was key to navigating the language during my time there.

This got me thinking about languages. When the Lord created the world, the people spoke one language. But because of their sin and arrogance to be like God, He created multiple languages to stop the sin in its track and to bring about humility in their confusion (Genesis 11:1-9).

Since He created all these languages, which one does He speak? He speaks one language: the saving gospel. Because of my sins, it's this one language that brings about humility amidst confusion (1 Corinthians 14:33), to stop sin in its track (1 John 2:1-3).

Thankfully, He doesn't leave me in my confusion but has sent a Helper in all things (John 14:15-17) whether in my personal Bible studies or my everyday activities. I am dependent on the Helper. He helps me to talk to the Lord (Romans 8:26). And He interprets what the Lord is saying to me (1 Corinthians 2:6-16). He is key to navigating the one language of God during my time here.

The one language He created was divided into many because of sin. Because of sin, He created one language to unite us back with Him. Why?

*****

"For God so loved the world, that He gave his only Son, that whoever believes in Him should not perish but have eternal life. For God did not send His Son into the world to condemn the world, but in order that the world might be saved through Him."
John 3:16-17 ESV

Challenge: Make a concerted effort to connect with someone. Reach out to an old friend that you have not talked to in a while. Make plans to get together with an acquaintance to develop that friendship.

W h a t   W a s   H e   T h i n k i n g

Depending on what's going on in my life, the emotions I feel when I read the horrific events of Jesus' cruel death vary. But whatever that emotion is, I've always experienced it as an outsider, a spectator at the cross. I "see" the screaming crowds. The soldiers spitting and beating Him. The people mocking and cursing Him. His best friend crying. Oh, His dear mother. It's so painful to read.

He said so little from His betrayal till death. What emotions He had to have experienced! I often wondered what He could be thinking at different times. And then I read Psalm 22.

It begins in complete anguish. This tortured soul is desperately grasping for His Father's helping hand. In tears, He feels alone. Trapped. Enduring agonizing pain. It's so painful to read. Hearing Him tell me these things makes me gasp for air. I am not worthy.

But, then there's a turn in emotion. He finds strength in His Father. His focus is again clear. More motivated. Absolutely commanding. He sees His victory! I see my victory in Him! My broken heart healed!

He never once asked "why?" Instead, He tells me why: "Posterity shall serve him; it shall be told of the Lord to the coming generation; they shall come and proclaim his righteousness to a people yet unborn, that he has done it." (30-31)

*****

"those who seek him shall praise the Lord! May your hearts live forever!"
Psalms 22:26

Challenge: Read Psalm 22 during the Lord's supper.

It's His

To become a Christian, I had to first have faith in Jesus Christ as the Son of God (Romans 10:17) before I could confess my faith (Romans 10:8-10). Then, I obeyed His command to be baptized for the forgiveness of my sins (Acts 2:38). Among many things, I am commanded to be faithful unto death (Revelation 2:10). And also, supplement my faith with virtue, knowledge, self-control, steadfastness, godliness, brotherly affection and love (2 Peter 1:5-7).

All this is absolutely essential to my salvation, but it's not what saves me. As blasphemous as this sounds, I really am praising the all righteous, ever patient God.

What, then, does save me? Faithfulness. Not my faithfulness that I just talked about, but His faithfulness. The Lord's faithfulness. Without it, He would not be God. And without God, there is no salvation! How, then, is He faithful?

First and foremost, He is **faithful** to His word (Hebrews 6:18).
And He **faithfully** waits for my repentance with patience. (2 Peter 3:9).
Without fail, He **faithfully** extends His mercy and grace (Hebrews 4:16).
He **faithfully** forgives my sins...constantly (1 John 1:9).
Lastly, He **faithfully** loves me (1 John 4:10).
His **faithfulness** is consistent, constant, & true (Malachi 3:6).
It is *HIS* faithfulness that saves me!

*****

"But this I call to mind, and therefore I have hope: The steadfast love of the Lord never ceases; his mercies never come to an end; they are new every morning; great is your faithfulness."
Lamentations 3:21-23 ESV

Challenge: Can you recall a time when His faithfulness carried you through a difficult time in your life? a good and happy time?

Sowing the seed of the gospel takes patience. More accurately, finding good soil to sow the seed takes patience. I scatter seed, but it's those seeds that grow on fertile ground that I'm looking for. I'm looking for Matthew!

Jesus traveled about doing exactly that. One day, not far from His hometown, He was about to pass by a tax collection booth. And there was Matthew, the tax collector. Sitting. I doubt he was getting much work done with Jesus and the crowd in town. What interests me is that Matthew wasn't in the crowd, wasn't asking for anything. Being a dreaded tax collector, was he avoiding the righteous Man? Was he thinking that he wasn't worthy to be near the Holy Healer?

Jesus passed his way. Rather than avoiding the dreaded tax collector, Jesus told him, "Follow Me". How did Matthew react? He got up and followed Him (Matthew 9:9)! And he invited all his friends over for dinner to meet Jesus, too (Luke 5:27-29). Jesus saw a sinner. A sinner who needed Him (Matthew 9:11-13). Matthew was fertile soil, a fertile soul.

As I travel about scattering the seed of the gospel, I pray I don't avoid the "dreaded tax collectors" but rather see all the Matthews out there, so I can say "Follow Him".

*****

"Do you not say, 'There are yet four months, then comes the harvest'? Look, I tell you, lift up your eyes, and see that the fields are white for harvest."
John 4:35

Challenge: Look for your Matthew. You could be passing his way.

W h o   i s   T h i s ?

Several times I've scrolled thru social media seeing movie stars, internet sensations, and pop singers and thought, "Who is this?" They've got cameras flashing, thousands of "likes", people screaming their names. And I'm still scrolling asking "Who is this?"

There was a great commotion in the city one day with lots of singing and shouting from large crowds. Imagine it - the whole city was stirred up! "And when He entered Jerusalem, the whole city was stirred up, saying, 'Who is this?'" Matthew 21:10. If they weren't the ones praising (vs. 9), they were the ones asking the question.

What a sight (and sound, too) that had to have been! I've been to parades, concerts, sports games. Crowds shouting and cheering for their idol can be so loud! I've been there, done that! I wonder what I would have been doing in that crowd. More importantly, what am I doing in my crowded city?

- Am I shouting "Hosanna to the Son of David! Blessed is he who comes in the name of the Lord! Hosanna in the highest!" (vs. 9)?
- Am I the joyful, healed sinner that proclaims Him as Christ with all my heart, soul, and mind, in word and deed, with meekness and fear so much so that the attention of people turn to Christ?
- Am I ready to answer the question, "Who is this?" (1 Peter 3:15). "This is Jesus, the prophet from Nazareth of Galilee" (vs. 11)!!

*****

"Clap your hands, all peoples! Shout to God with loud songs of joy! For the Lord, the Most High, is to be feared, a great king over all the earth."
Psalms 47:1-2

Challenge: Tell someone about Jesus. It doesn't have to be a long conversation, or even a Bible study. But pray that it becomes one.

Come Here, You!

I remember one incident (actually several incidents) when my sister and I were at each other, annoying and fighting against each other. We were so caught up in ourselves that we didn't realize how that had traveled through our house to where our dad could hear. "Come here, you two!" Uh-oh! We went from at each other's throats to tightly bonded together. We were gonna get it!

I had that same reaction this morning when I read Numbers 12. Miriam and Aaron were talking about Moses' foreign wife. Their problem wasn't really with his wife but with Moses himself. They wanted to be leader, the one in charge, the one who spoke with God. I can hear them now getting all riled up, angering one another with every word they spoke, justifying themselves. What they didn't realize was that God heard them. "Come out, you three, to the tent of meeting." (vs. 14). I know *exactly* how they were feeling!! They were gonna get it!

They went from fussing and fighting against other to tightly bonded together. In the tent, Miriam was struck with leprosy (vs. 10). Seeing their sister in such a horrific state, they pleaded with God. Aaron confessed their sin. And Moses, who could've easily said, "ha, that's what you get", instead desperately cried, "O God, please heal her— please." (vs. 13).

The Holy Spirit described Moses in vs. 3 as, "very meek, more than all people who were on the face of the earth." What an example to leave me! It is my prayer to be very meek when a brother does me wrong. It is my prayer that I desperately cry out to the Lord to heal a sister's sin when I could easily say, "ha, that's what you get!" And I pray that I'm never so caught up in myself that I forget we're following the Lord together through this wilderness of life!

*****

"Let no corrupting talk come out of your mouths, but only such as is good for building up, as fits the occasion, that it may give grace to those who hear. And do not grieve the Holy Spirit of God, by whom you were sealed for the day of redemption. Let all bitterness and wrath and anger and clamor and slander be put away from you, along with all malice. Be kind to one another, tenderhearted, forgiving one another, as God in Christ forgave you."
Ephesians 4:29-32 ESV

Challenge: Meekness is defined: The quality or state of being meek: a mild, moderate, humble, or submissive quality (Merriam-Webster.com). It has been described as "strength under control; power to do anything but kept under control to do the right thing". In what areas of your life can you improve and become more meek?

_____

_____

_____

_____

_____

W h y   N u m b e r s ?

I just read chapter 1 of Numbers. I kept asking myself, what is the Lord trying to teach me? It's not addition. Maybe some history? Maybe the ancestral line? Or the great number of people?

Then I thought maybe I should learn and understand the duties of the Levites and their responsibilities of the Tabernacle. They were to care for it and its furnishings, set it up and break it down, etc. Nah, maybe not. Why do I need to learn Numbers?

But then I read the answer to my question: "Thus did the people of Israel; they did according to all that the Lord commanded Moses." (vs. 54).

So many times thru the years I've bogged myself down with "why" rather than doing "according to all the Lord commanded." I was like my kids, "why do I need to make my bed? Why do I need to eat vegetables? Why, why, why?"

It's not at all wrong to question why I should worship on the first day of the week or to love my neighbor as myself or many other things. That's how I will grow as a child of God. But sometimes, it's peaceful to just say "Yes, Lord, Your will be done".

****

And a voice came out of the cloud, saying, "This is My beloved Son. Hear Him!"
Luke 9:35 NKJV

Challenge: Pray fervently to God. And....GIVE IT TO HIM!

Reunion

My older son, who lives out of state, decided a few months back to surprise his younger brother. He wanted to help him move into his dorm for the first time. As each day passed, I got more and more excited for the reunion. We decided to meet at a restaurant, with him already there waiting for us to arrive. As we walked toward the door, he walked out, arms out with a big smile on his face! His brother was so surprised! I was in pure joy, not only for the surprise but to have my family together, whole. There may have been a tear or two or a lot, maybe.

It reminded me of another reunion that's planned, but it's not a total surprise (Matthew 25:1-13). As each day passes, I get more and more excited. The plan is to meet in the clouds where the Lord is waiting to greet me (1 Thessalonians 4:15-17). I imagine Him with His arms open wide with a big smile on His face. He will wipe away my tears, and I will live in pure joy (Revelation 21:4). His family will finally be together, whole (Mark 3:34-35).

I love my sons with *all* my heart. And the reunion with them made my heart want to burst from love and happiness! I didn't want our time together to end. And because I love the Lord with all my heart, soul, mind, and strength (Mark 12:30), the final reunion with Him will be everlasting, with no more goodbyes, no more mourning, no more sadness (Revelation 21:4), where my time with Him and my spiritual family will never end!

***

He who testifies to these things says, "Surely I am coming soon."
Amen. Come, Lord Jesus!
Revelation 22:20 ESV

Challenge: Are you ready? Are you looking forward to the reunion? Read Revelation 21 and 22.

My Calendar's Full

I've got to work. Then, I have to get groceries. Bring the kids to karate and wrestling. Or is it football and orchestra? I can't forget the PTA meeting. I signed up for cupcakes for the class party. Need to bake those! After that, I've got to cook dinner, make sure kids get cleaned up then off to bed. Oh wait, homework! Clean the kitchen. Spend a few minutes with my hubby, basically to see which of us falls asleep the quickest. He wins every time! As the ever defeated sleepyhead, I load the washer and fold what's in the dryer. I'll iron tomorrow.

This was me years ago. My time to spend with God was limited: reading the Bible with my preschool class I taught, studying in Bible class two times a week, and praying while falling asleep. The Lord knew I was busy in my short 24 hours, right? I wanted to devote time and energy to serve and teach His gospel, but how, when my responsibilities kept me busy, to say the least, or overwhelmed, at its worst.

Once I made a conscious decision to put God first, "stuff" fell into place and was prioritized more easily. I had to decide what was more important: busy-ness or holiness. Those things that kept my calendar full and my gas tank empty were fruitless in the kingdom UNTIL I finally opened my eyes to see all the opportunities that God placed in front of me.

A fellow wrestling mom seeking peace in her chaotic world was opened for a Bible study. The lag time waiting for one practice to finish before heading to another was a perfect time to pray. Baking extra cupcakes to give out with a little note or a hug were opportunities to shine my Christian light. Quick dinners were still precious family time when we played "High/Low" (a game to recall our day and its blessings). Bedtimes were special prayer times with my kids. And so, *so much more*!!

Jesus said, "But seek first the kingdom of God and his righteousness, and all these things will be added to you" (Matthew 6:33). Making the decision to obey this command didn't free up my calendar. Instead, with each flip of the full page, He's making me into a better servant of His.

*****

"Do not be conformed to this world, but be transformed by the renewal of your mind, that by testing you may discern what is the will of God, what is good and acceptable and perfect."
Romans 12:2 ESV

Challenge: Look at your calendar. Pencil in where seeking His righteousness will "let your light shine before others, so that they may see your good works and give glory to your Father who is in Heaven." Matthew 5:16

In the Stink of It

When my kids were little, we went to the zoo. As we turned the corner to head toward the elephants for their show, there was a smell that just about knocked me over. It provoked dry heaves from my younger son. It was horrible! It was coming from one of the exotic animals. Racing through that area to get to the elephant corral was no better! Those enormous beasts were just as smelly. How do the zoo keepers stand that smell? I couldn't be paid enough to work there. I can't take it when my own dog stinks!

Imagine caring for these animals day in and day out. Feeding them. My dog's food stinks. What would a hippo's food smell like? And cleaning after them. Ewww! What would be worse is keeping them confined to a small corral, pen, or cubby and having little air circulation.

Remember Noah? All these animals and more in an ark. The stink of the animals. The stink of their food. The stink of their corrals, pens, and cubbies. In an ark, that he built while being mocked, that had one small window that couldn't be opened for some fresh air because of the water falling from the sky! In this rocking ark, with the noises and smells, wondering when the waters would subside and be able to walk on solid ground again. In this ark with his family, the only living humans that will exist after God opens the door.

Faith! Faith! Faith! It was his faith in God that got him through it all: the mocking, the stink, the rocking. Because of his faith in the Savior, he endured to salvation (Genesis 9:1)

And it must be my faith in God that'll get me through it all, too (Hebrews 11:6): the mocking of unbelievers (Matthew 5:10-12), the stink of sin (Proverbs 6:12-15), the rocking trials of life (Mark 11:22). But in my ark of faith in the Savior, I can endure to salvation (Matthew 24:13).

*****

"For I consider that the sufferings of this present time are not worth comparing with the glory that is to be revealed to us."
Romans 8:18

Challenge: What has your ark of faith in the Savior carried you through?

Ponder

When I am troubled.

When I am sad.

When I am confused.

When I am broken.

When I am calm.

When I am content.

When I am joyful.

When I am praising.

*****

"I will ponder all your work, and meditate on your mighty deeds."
Psalm 77:12

Challenge: Start a blessings journal. Whether you take a few minutes before bed at night or in the morning to recall the day before's blessings, write them down. You can also carry a small notepad around with you to write down blessings that you just received. Write them in your journal later.

One Day

We have sea turtle nests in Florida. They're roped off and protected during the entire incubation period. I've never seen them hatch and crawl back out to sea to live long lives. Several times I've tried, but I haven't been able to experience it yet. With my camera ready for pictures and the video on my phone ready to record this really exciting time, I always go hoping that today is the day. I have taken pictures of the roped off area. I've brought friends to see it, too. But no big event yet! I'll keep going back with my camera because one day I will see them! I just know it!

That's life as a Christian. One day I'll be able to enjoy a very big event. The day I get to go to heaven! Until then, I'll be ready and prepared. And I'll keep bringing friends to show them what they can have: the chance to live an eternal life, too. I'll keep returning to the Lord after my mistakes because I know that there is a life waiting for me that's far better than this one. He said so! Until then, my salvation is protected in the cross.

*****

"For in this hope we were saved. Now hope that is seen is not hope. For who hopes for what he sees? But if we hope for what we do not see, we wait for it with patience."
Romans 8:24-25 ESV

Challenge: Read the epistle of James

Dark Blessings

How dark, sad, and dreadful Psalm 79 is! Twelve verses of bloodshed, defilement of God's temple, taunting & mocking, vicious deaths, anger, groaning, & pain. It's terrible!

When it seemed like there was no more hope, Asaph, in this dark time, humbled himself, thanked God, and praised Him. In verse 13, he ended this Psalm with 11 blessings that I counted.

"**But**" - Asaph knew the Lord would hear his plea. There was still light in this dark time: God.

"**we your people,**" - he knew the Lord still loved His people.

"**the sheep**" - sheep wander but end up following the Shepherd, the One who cares for them because He loves them.

"**of your pasture,**" - where all blessings are and where we could feed to our fill.

"**will**" - the faith & hope in the Lord to provide relief.

"**give thanks**" - because he knows the Lord will provide.

"**to you forever;**" - the eternal God

"**from generation to generation**" - we are the finite ones, not the Lord nor His power.

"**we will**" - the hope of being forgiven

"**recount**" ("show forth" NKJV) - able to keep vows of faithfulness because of His mercy and grace.

"**your praise**" - because we are forgiven people.
Psalms 79:13 ESV

*****

"And I prayed to the Lord my God, and made confession, and said, "O Lord, great and awesome God, who keeps His covenant and mercy with those who love Him, and with those who keep His commandments,"
Daniel 9:4 NKJV

Challenge: Read Psalm 79. Be sure your blessings journal is up to date.

That Alarm!

After a sleepless night, I decided I needed an afternoon coffee, nitro at that. I placed my order and headed to the window to receive my grande cup of happy. As I waited for the few cars ahead of me to leave, I heard an alarm. It was not like the common car alarm. It was a repetitive warning sound and very, very loud. I rolled down my windows & looked around. No one else was looking for it. There's no way I could be the only person in this area to hear this! Traffic kept flowing. People in the nearby strip mall continued walking. We could be under attack right now and everyone was just going about their business as usual. I felt like I was in an Alfred Hitchcock movie. The sound finally stopped. And I got my coffee wondering if I had just imagined it.

This is it! This is how it is! The alarm sounds (Acts 2:38). It's a repetitive warning (Deuteronomy 32:46; Ezekiel 3:16-21; Revelation 22:18-19). And it's very, very loud (Galatians 5:19-24)! But who's looking for it? And who's going about their business as usual? It's not a movie or my imagination. It's day to day life!

But one day, when that trumpet blasts loudly (1 Thessalonians 4:16), every single one will hear it (1 Corinthians 15:52). Some will try to scatter. Others will try to hide (Revelation 6:16-17). Then it'll finally stop (Matthew 24:29-31).

*****

for it is written, "As I live, says the Lord, every knee shall bow to me, and every tongue shall confess to God." So then each of us will give an account of himself to God.
Romans 14:11-12 ESV

Challenge: Start a prayer journal. Write down specifics. After some time, go back and marvel at His answers.

Proverbs 8

Wisdom is beautiful.
Wisdom is precious and valuable.

Wisdom is safe.
Wisdom is established and sacred.

Wisdom is delightful.
Wisdom is generous and honest.

Wisdom is life.
Wisdom is God.

*****

"Who has put wisdom in the inward parts or given understanding to the mind?"
Job 38:36

Challenge: Read Job chapters 38 and 39

Lagniappe

/lan'yap/

n. Something given as a bonus
or extra gift
(commonly used by the natives of New Orleans)

Adoption

Back in January 2005, there was a story of a three year old adopted boy who was given back to his birth mother. This is not the first time a story like this has been reported. Hearing this story made me think of our spiritual adoption to God, our Father.

Here was a three year boy who was adopted at birth by a married couple. Life was good. Everyone was happy. Then, the birth mother, coaxed by the birth father to whom she was not married, decided that she wanted custody of this child. Because of a loop hole in the adoption process, the boy was returned to her.

The birth grandmother, in a television interview, stated that she supports the adoptive parents. She had also stated that her daughter had expressed to her that the young boy has a better life with them (the adoptive parents). What she could not understand was why she would seek custody after all this time. She continued with accusations that the birth father has abused her daughter. The daughter has since ceased communication with her for several months. [Today Show, January 17, 2005]

In an interview shown later in the show, the adoptive parents discussed their ordeal. A video showed the heart retching farewell between the parents and the child. The mother stated that preparing to give the child back was "like preparing for his death." She later expressed concern because there were several occasions when the child talked about taking pills and being slapped after visits with the birth parents. Reports to authorities went unnoticed. They stated that they are not giving up the fight to get him back, that they are not giving up easily. As of this writing, the adoptive parents have 2 appeals in the case.

After hearing this story, I kept thinking about our Heavenly Father, and how we are His adopted children (Ephesians 1:5). This is a very simple view of how the Lord feels about our return to sin. We are His adopted child through our new birth (John 3:3-6). Life is good.

We are happy. Then, the evil forces coaxed by Satan decide that he wants to take back custody of our soul. Because of a loop hole, we succumb. We are all familiar with the loop holes: "everyone is doing it", "just this one time won't hurt", "I can always go back", "that's how you interpret it".

In the back of our minds is that little voice telling us that our life was better with our adopted Father; asking us why are we doing this? Some of us even cut off communication with that little voice (1Timothy 4:1-2).

The Lord had told us how He feels about the whole situation (2Peter 3:9). There is no need for a video to be shown; He wrote a book. He is not easily giving up on getting us back (Luke 19:10). For those of us who do return to the Lord in repentance (2 Corinthians 7:10), there is joy in Heaven (Luke 15:7). The Lord knows about the visits with the father of this world. He knows of the abuse we choose to endure (Hebrews 4:15). Yet, He gladly and willingly takes us back (Luke 15).

As His adopted children, we are given the privilege to have an abundant life (John 10:10). We are members of one body, one family, the church (1Corinthians 12:12). If our adopted brothers/ sisters are making visits to the father of this world, we know our reports will not go unnoticed, our prayers unheard. We cannot just sit back, throw out a loop hole, and hope that "this one time won't hurt", "he can always come back". That would be like "preparing for his/her death." We have put on Christ (Galatians 3:27), therefore, we must seek the lost (Luke 19:10). Let us stand up to the charge laid in front of us: "Stand fast therefore in the liberty wherewith Christ hath made us free, and be not entangled again with the yoke of bondage." (Galatians 5:1). As of this writing, the Lord has many appeals in our case.

I AM

Exodus 3:6-15

6 Moreover He said, "I am the God of your father—the God of Abraham, the God of Isaac, and the God of Jacob." And Moses hid his face, for he was afraid to look upon God. 7 And the Lord said: "I have surely seen the oppression of My people who are in Egypt, and have heard their cry because of their taskmasters, for I know their sorrows. 8 So I have come down to deliver them out of the hand of the Egyptians, and to bring them up from that land to a good and large land, to a land flowing with milk and honey, to the place of the Canaanites and the Hittites and the Amorites and the Perizzites and the Hivites and the Jebusites. 9 Now therefore, behold, the cry of the children of Israel has come to Me, and I have also seen the oppression with which the Egyptians oppress them.
10 Come now, therefore, and I will send you to Pharaoh that you may bring My people, the children of Israel, out of Egypt."

11 But Moses said to God, "Who am I that I should go to Pharaoh, and that I should bring the children of Israel out of Egypt?" 12 So He said, "I will certainly be with you. And this shall be a sign to you that I have sent you: When you have brought the people out of Egypt, you shall serve God on this mountain."

13 Then Moses said to God, "Indeed, when I come to the children of Israel and say to them, 'The God of your fathers has sent me to you,' and they say to me, 'What is His name?' what shall I say to them?"

14 And God said to Moses, "I AM WHO I AM." And He said, "Thus you shall say to the children of Israel, 'I AM has sent me to you.'"
15 Moreover God said to Moses, "Thus you shall say to the children of Israel: 'The Lord God of your fathers, the God of Abraham, the God of Isaac, and the God of Jacob, has sent me to you. This is My name forever, and this is My memorial to all generations.'

I AM....
- the same God that was with Abraham, Isaac, and Jacob - 430 yrs ago
- the same God that is with you now and will certainly continue to be with you (v. 12)
- faithful in fulfilling my promises to Abraham, Isaac, Jacob
- deliverer of My people - saving them from bondage (v. 8, 9)
- compassionate - have seen the oppression; heard their cry; know their sorrow (v. 7)
- relief, rest and hope.... because of that
- to be remembered and worshipped FOREVER - a memorial to all generations (v. 15)

Jesus declared "I AM" in John 8:58 - what was He saying? He was letting His people know that:

I AM...
- deliverer of My people - Galatians 1:4.
- to be remembered - 1Corinthians 11:24-25
- to be loved - John 15:9 .... why?
- because I have always loved you - 1 John 4:19

The great I AM came to Earth as a man. The same great I AM, who had seen the oppression, heard the cries, and had known the sorrows of His people, came to live as a man. To be tempted as a man. To share in the same desires and emotions that we have.
Hebrews 4:15 - *For we do not have a High Priest who cannot sympathize with our weaknesses, but was in all points tempted as we are, yet without sin.*
Why? To comfort and encourage and motivate us. He didn't live life like us for HIS benefit!

The value of something is determined by what someone is willing to pay for it. What is the value of sin? Romans 6:23 says sin is worth death. We pay for sin with our soul. But the great I AM bought it back. He thinks we are very valuable. To Him, our soul's value is worth His death.

He redeemed our souls so He can return it back to the great I AM. Ecclesiastes 12:7 *"Then the dust will return to the earth as it was, And the spirit will return to God who gave it."*

He gave our souls to us. We sold it for sin. He bought it back at a far more valuable cost so He can keep it forever.
May we always remember 1 John 4:19
"We love Him because He first loved us."

You are Barnabas!

You are a Barnabas!! Did you know that? We are all Barnabas! How do I know that? The Bible said so.

Genesis 1:27 - "So God created man in his own image, in the image of God he created him; male and female he created them."
vs. 31 "And God saw everything that he had made, and behold, it was VERY GOOD."

He created us. And it was VERY GOOD. He told mankind to be fruitful and multiply and fill the earth and subdue it. God had specific plans for mankind.

James 1 starting at vs. 18 - "Of his own will he brought us forth by the word of truth, that we should be a kind of firstfruits of his creatures. (22) But be doers of the word, and not hearers only deceiving yourselves. (25) But the one who looks into the perfect law, the law of liberty, and perseveres, being no hearer who forgets but a doer who acts, he will be blessed in his doing."

He's got specific plans for us - be DOERS of the word!

But, does that make me a Barnabas? Paul is telling the church in Thessalonica ch. 5 to be aware, be sober, put on the breastplate of faith and love, and the helmet of salvation because God is coming for you. He is coming to get HIS people! YOU! ME! Because of this, comfort (encourage) one another and edify (build up) one another, just as you are doing.

Why should we comfort/encourage and edify/build up one another? Because, as my 18 year old newly college son just told me, "Adulting is hard!" "Being a Christian in this world is hard!" We need comfort, encouragement, edification, building up. We need each other.

When we come back from "adulting" (being a Christian) in this world, sometimes we come back battered, bruised, discouraged, hurt, sad. We need each other. Our awesome God in all His wisdom created His church, a safe haven, a refuge. He knew that we could give each other the comfort and building up that we need.

So how exactly can we be the Barnabas that we are meant to be? First, let's see why he was called "Son of Encouragement" by the apostles. I found several reasons, but here are three.

1. ACTS 9 - Barnabas stepped up and personally took Paul to the apostles and declared to them about Paul's conversion when no one else would accept Paul.

Barnabas was a Christian of good reputation.

Can your sisters count on you? Can a sister come to you in her time of need? Maybe because she's hurting in her marriage. What about the woman overwhelmed with doctrine because she's a new Christian; another is spiritually injured, and another is a lonely widow, or any other problem this life hands us.

In his challenging time, Paul needed a Christian who was full of the Holy Spirit and of faith (Acts 11:24). He had Barnabas.

2. ACTS 11 - After the dispersion of Jews because of Stephen's death, the apostles sent Barnabas to Antioch because these Jews were preaching to Gentiles. In verse 23, "When he came and saw the grace of God, he was glad and he exhorted them all to remain faithful to the Lord with steadfast purpose."

The grace of God made him glad.

Do you rejoice with the angels when a sinner repents, even for the woman who had a less-than-church life? Does your heart rejoice when a sister confesses a sin...again...because she continually struggles?

Christians were offering the gospel's saving grace to the Hellenists, Greeks. GENTILES were being saved! Barnabas was glad! He exhorted (strongly urged) them to remain faithful. It was here in Antioch that they were first called Christians.

3. Thru ACTS 12-15 - he boldly preached and did many signs and wonders right along side Paul.

He boldly preached and taught with a brother.

Are you bold? Do you invite your hair stylist, the server at your favorite restaurant, your doctor, the person behind you in Starbucks to Bible class or worship? Do you have personal Bible studies? Do you door knock?

I read in a book years ago that Christians are Earth movers. Think about that. Earth moving equipment, such as bulldozers, excavators, trenchers, (equipment that used to send my sons into a tizzy!) can do BIG work:
- drill through a mountain in Colorado or one of those Sequoia trees in California to build a road.
- build up land barriers on the east coast and barrier islands in southern Louisiana to protect against storm surges
- haul off dirt and muck and boulders

Earth movers change landscapes. *Be an earth mover* - show God's love! This world certainly needs it. Drill holes through barriers then build a road to eternal friendship. Build up (edify) to strengthen each other when life's storm-surges pound us. Haul off the dirt and muck and the boulders that weigh us down by using encouragement! Here are some landscapers in the Bible.
- Caleb & Joshua encouraged Moses to overtake the Promised land (Numbers 13 & 14).They were the only ones of that generation to enter.
- Moses, in turn, encouraged & strengthened Joshua to lead (Deuteronomy 3:28)
- Mordecai built up and encouraged Esther to talk to the king - it saved an entire race of people (Book of Esther)
- Onesiphorus sought out and refreshed Paul while he was in prison. (2 Timothy 1:16-17)
- Paul encouraged Timothy throughout both letters.
- Paul also encouraged Titus in his letter, particularly 2:15
- Jesus to His apostles - "I am with you always" Matthew 28:20

Be a Barnabas - be a daughter of encouragement - **WHY?**

Paul tells us why starting 1 Timothy 4:6 - (Emphasis mine)
"If you instruct the brethren in these things, **you will be a good minister of Jesus Christ**, nourished in the words of faith and of the good doctrine which you have carefully followed"....he goes on to say that.... "godliness is profitable for **all things**".... He continues in verse 11 "These things command and teach. Let no one despise your youth, but **be an example** to the believers in word, in conduct, in love, in spirit, in faith, in purity. Till I come, give attention to **reading**, to **exhortation**, to **doctrine**." Verse 15 "Meditate on these things; give yourself entirely to them, that your progress may be evident to all. Take heed to yourself and to the doctrine. Continue in them, for in doing this <u>you will save both yourself and those who hear you.</u>"

Be an earth moving daughter of encouragement - **HOW?** How can we change the landscape?

<u>Get to know your spiritual family</u> - You can't encourage who you don't know. Spend time together. Pencil in your calendar one or two a times a week or month as long as it's intentional, to go grab lunch, or coffee with a sister in Christ. Too shy? or new to a congregation? or a new Christian? or simply new to doing this? Go with more than the two of you to help the conversation along. Get to know your eternal family!

While you're at it, do the same with a neighbor, co-worker, your child's friend's parent. You can set a goal. By the end of this year, you'll get to know 1, 3, 5 new people. Be intentional to break thru barriers with the goal of building an eternal friendship.

<u>Pray together</u> - set aside time to pray each day or several times a week. A few of us here at South Florida Avenue church of Christ, try to pray several times a week. Pray about specifics. It'll strengthen your relationship with God. It'll strengthen your relationship with each other as you both approach the throne of God together. Look what it did for the 1st century church!

When you're out in a restaurant with your new friend, ask if it's ok to pray. I've never had anyone turn me down. You lead the prayer. Also, ask your server if there is anything that they'd like for you to pray for them. It opens doors and presents opportunities.
Pray fervently for one another, James 5:16

Be a mentor - not an official title, but offer or accept a request to teach something you're good at: organizing meals, visiting or calling, helping a new mom, how to meet new people, how to have a Bible study. The possibilities are endless. Help someone tap into a talent that could be hidden within them. Help others get out of their comfort zones and to work in the kingdom. I am so thankful I had people in my Christian walk that taught me what, how, & why to serve in the kingdom.

Older ladies, 1 Timothy 5:2 I exhort you as mothers, teach me! I'm an empty nester now. I want to be a better servant of God in this new season of my life. Younger women, Titus 2:3-5, I've been where you are. Let me help guide you. If we don't do these things, we are denying ourselves of blessings.

Read & study together - not just Sundays or Wednesdays but outside of this building. Here is something that several of us here at South Florida Avenue church of Christ do: ask someone (or two) to read a book of the Bible with you. Read a chapter a day at your own convenience. Then you text each other about something you learned from that chapter, or maybe a question about it. It holds each of you accountable to reading and studying. Remember what Paul said : give attention to reading, to doctrine.

Also outside of this building, host a study group in your home with neighbors, co-workers, your child's friend's parent. Choose an epistle like James or Philippians and study it. Use your Bible class notes or sermon notes. If you don't feel comfortable with that, there are so many great reliable faithful resources available. Plant & water the seed. 1 Corinthians 3:6

Listen to announcements - this is a BIG one! Write them down or grab a bulletin and follow up. Go visit in the hospital - call or send card if you can't visit. Offer to drive to an upcoming doctor's appointment. Send a card to the youth group for their recent devo/service project. Be aware and intentional. Matthew 13:43 *"Then the righteous will shine forth as the sun in the kingdom of their Father. He who has ears to hear, let him hear!"*

Visit a shut-in - one of our shut-ins asked the youth group and their parents to pray that she's not so lonesome. She recently told me, "I'm so glad I haven't been forgotten."
"I was sick and you visited Me; I was in prison and you came to Me." Matthew 25:36

Look for visitors - Another BIG one! Tag team with someone, whether your husband, family member or another sister in your congregation. Be sure to seek out your visitors with the intent of meeting them. Then introduce them to your tag teamer. If possible, sit with your visitor. Or invite them to lunch or coffee. REMEMBER THEIR NAMES! Our 2nd visit to South Florida Avenue church of Christ, the Associate Minister came up to us in the parking lot and greeted us by name. I was floored! It left a lasting impression on my family and me.

If you are a new member to your congregation, you can do this, too! Introduce yourself. If they happen to be a member, simply let them know that you are new and you haven't met yet and are now glad to have met. If you have never done this before because you might be shy, tell the visitor exactly that. You'd be surprise what an ice breaker that is!! For BOTH of you!!

Let's show our visitors that the church is a refuge for them, too!

What else? - say THANK YOU! These 2 words are such motivators! Give a "great job" card to the boys who pick up attendance cards or opens doors. Leave "I appreciate all you do" cards in classrooms for your Bible class teachers. Tell the song leader thank you. Thank your elders for their prayers - and pray for them. Don't just thank your preacher for a great Biblically sound sermon he preached - apply it to your life. How about asking your deacons how you can help. Support a member's business - ask if you can post it on social media. Acknowledge birthdays & special accomplishments. Attend one of the kids recital or play. These ideas are only the tip of the spiritual iceberg!

Senior Ladies, you are not exempt. I once had a older lady tell me that she is passing the Christian torch on to the younger generation. I had only been a Christian for a little while. I thought this was great and how it was done. Psalms 92:12-14 says the righteous must still bear fruit in old age.

"And let us not grow weary of doing good, for in due season we will reap, IF we do not lose heart. Therefore, as we have opportunity, let us do good to all, especially to those who are of the household of faith." Galatians 6: 9-10

Since we were created in God's image:
- we want to be loved (John 3:16)
- we want to be heard (Luke 9:35)
- we want friends (John 15:15)
- we want to be cared for (Matthew 23:37)
- we want all of this reciprocated (1 John 4:19)

We have been created in His image. We have been saved by the blood of Jesus Christ. We are continually taught by the Holy Spirit. Can you think of a better way to say thank you than to be His child and to desire EVERYONE to join you in Heaven?

So, you, my sisters in Christ, go move His earth!
Go, my sisters of encouragement, change the landscapes around you!
Go, my fellow Barnabas, fulfill the Lord's command to be fruitful with the fruit of the Spirit. Multiply and fill the earth with them.

"I can do all things through Christ which strengthens me." Philippians 4:13

As Paul, Silvanus and Timothy told the church in Thessalonica, "we exhorted each one of you and encouraged you and charged you to walk in a manner worthy of God, who calls you into his own kingdom and glory."

Made in the USA
Lexington, KY
13 November 2019